The Broken Egg

A story to help children cope with the loss of a younger sibling

Joe Sutherland

AuthorHouse™
1663 Liberty Drive
Bloomington, IN 47403
www.authorhouse.com
Phone: 833-262-8899

This book is printed on acid-free paper.

ISBN: 978-1-4490-8347-2 (sc)

Library of Congress Control Number: 2010901966

Print information available on the last page.

Published by AuthorHouse 01/13/2022

authorHOUSE®

Little Dino Dean was so excited................
his Mommy had just laid an egg. He was going
to be a BIG Brother!!!

Soon Little Dino Dean would be able to play all kinds of games with his new baby brother or sister.

They would be able to play baseball together-

Maybe they would have tea with the Queen!

They could plant a big garden..........

.....or even go for a swim.

Maybe they would go on long walks and Little Dino Dean could teach the baby all about their home.

They could just lay around watching the clouds!

Little Dino Dean was so happy!!!

One day Mommy and Daddy Dinosaur called
Little Dino Dean to the nest.

They had some bad news that they had to tell him.

There would be no baby brother or sister- the egg was broken!

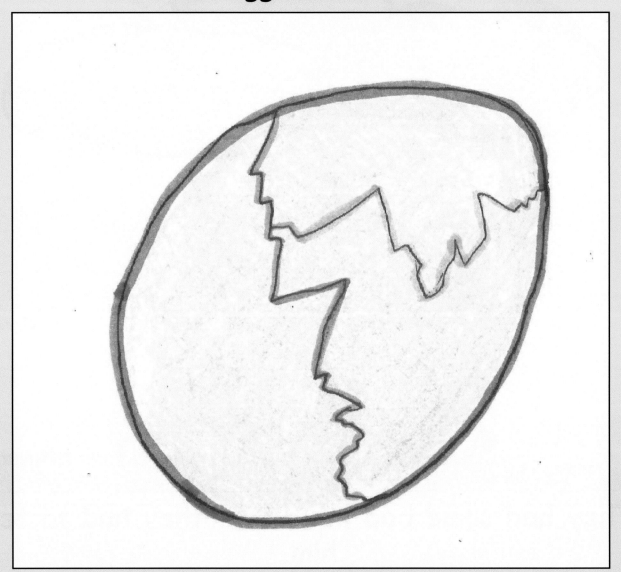

Mommy and Daddy Dinosaur gave Little Dino Dean a BIG hug.

Mommy and Daddy Dinosaur told Little Dino Dean how the little egg would not be a baby brother or sister.

There would be no games, no walks and
no watching the clouds go by..........

Little Dino Dean was very sad!

Mommy and Daddy Dinosaur wiped Little Dino Dean's tears and told him it was OK to be sad.

The little egg would not be with him as a little brother or sister, but the little egg would always be with Little Dino Dean........

.....in his heart!

As long as Little Dino Dean remembered
the egg it would always be there with him
whenever he played a game, went for a walk or
watched the clouds.

No matter what happens to our little eggs as long as we remember them and love them for who they were they will always be our little brothers, sisters, sons and daughters forever!

Printed in the United States
by Baker & Taylor Publisher Services